What's Opposite?

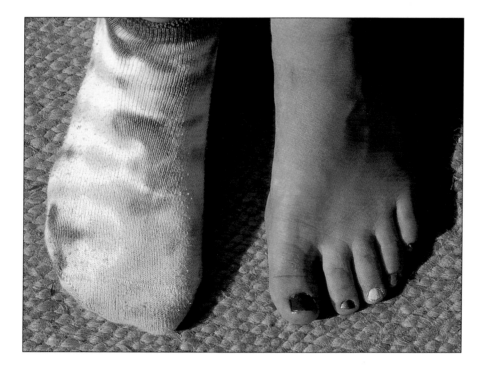

Stephen R. Swinburne

Boyds Mills Press

Foreword

Do you know that all day long you're surrounded by opposites? An opposite is a person or thing that is completely different from another. Some of your friends at school are sloppy, and some are neat. They are opposite. Some doors in your house are open, while others are closed. The milk jug in the refrigerator might be full, or it might be empty. It's easy to take opposites for granted.

But what if you lived in a world where everything was the same—a world with no opposites? Instead of hot and cold, your drink was medium. Instead of tall and short, every kid in your school was average in height. What would you do without frosty, cold drinks in the summer and piping-hot drinks in the winter? How interesting would a basketball game be with basketball players all the same height?

Opposites keep your days lively and interesting. Have fun guessing the opposites found in this book. The opposite of stop is go. Go for it!

—Steve Swinburne

An opposite is something
completely different from another thing.

Some children live in the country.

Some children live in the city.
Country and city are opposites.

Sitting is the opposite of standing.

When two things are related
but are as different as can be, they are opposite.

The opposite of winter . . .

. . . is summer.

Cars and trucks on the highway
go in opposite directions.

The opposite of a clean hand is a dirty hand.

Opposites are all around us: in and out.

Whole and smashed.

Top and bottom.

Knowing opposites is fun. What's the opposite of dry?

Wet.

What's the opposite of heavy?

Light.

What's the opposite of leaning?

Standing up straight.

What's the opposite of full?

Empty.

What's the opposite of a few apples?

Many apples.

What's the opposite of eyes closed?

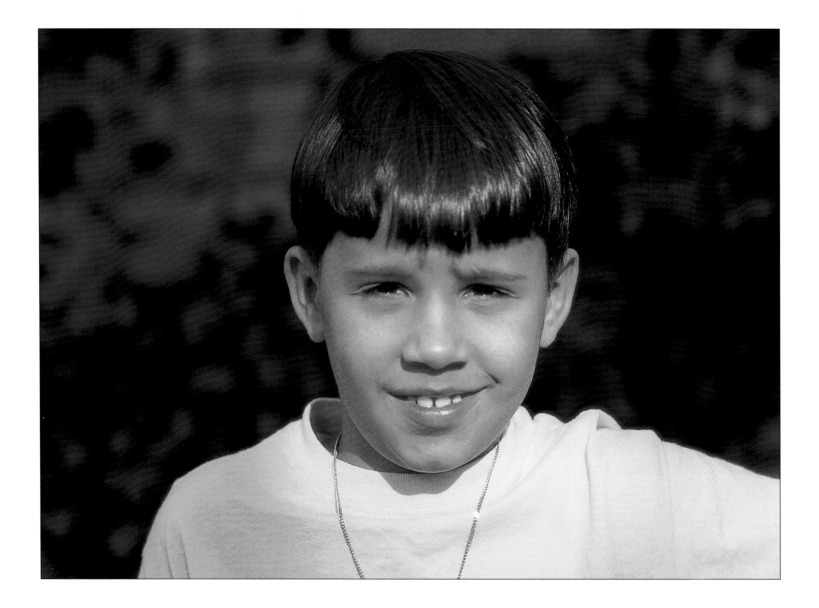

Eyes open.

What's the opposite of sweet?

Sour.

As you go through your day,
look closely for all the opposites around you.

You can find them everywhere.

Sometimes opposites make the best match.

Dedicated to all the different peoples of the planet
who are not opposite but really all the same

Acknowledgments

Thanks to the patient models who kept smiling after I'd said for the tenth time, "Just one more":
Kitt Sikes and Brooke Sabol (cover); Hayley and Devon Swinburne, Jocelin and Elisha Ruiz, Skylar Lewis,
Clarissa Rae Vanness, Colby Hescock, Logan Given, Jared Gundry, Heather Ishu, Mark Lee, Carlos Martinez,
Carmia Burrell, John and Matthew Streeter; the big hand of Keith Evans, and the small hand of Chloe Evans.
Thanks to Jessie Pomeroy for the 1952 John Deere M big and small tractors.

Text and illustrations copyright © 2000 by Stephen R. Swinburne
All rights reserved

Published by Caroline House • Boyds Mills Press, Inc. • A Highlights Company
815 Church Street • Honesdale, Pennsylvania 18431
Printed in Hong Kong

U.S. Cataloging-in-Publication Data (Library of Congress Standards)
Swinburne, Stephen R.
What's opposite? / by Stephen R. Swinburne.—1st ed. • [32]p. : col. ill. ; cm.
Summary: A photographic essay depicting opposites.
Hardcover ISBN 1-56397-881-4
Paperback ISBN 1-56397-905-5
1. English language — Synonyms and antonyms. 2. Opposites — Nonfiction.
I. Title.
428.1 [E] —21 2000 AC CIP
99-68095

First edition, 2000
Book designed by Randall Llewellyn • The text of this book is set in 24-point Garamond Light.

10 9 8 7 6 5 4 hc
10 9 8 7 6 5 4 pbk